Original title:
Cathedrals of Creativity

Copyright © 2024 Creative Arts Management OÜ
All rights reserved.

Author: Tim Wood
ISBN HARDBACK: 978-9916-88-050-0
ISBN PAPERBACK: 978-9916-88-051-7

Sanctuaries of Imagination

In the quiet corners of the mind,
Where dreams and visions intertwine,
A world unfolds, so pure and bright,
In shadows, tales take flight.

Colors swirl, realities bend,
Each thought a path, no need to end,
We wander realms both near and far,
Boundless wonders, our guiding star.

Echoes of whispers softly call,
In this haven, we rise or fall,
With open hearts, we paint the skies,
In sanctuaries where magic lies.

The Archways of Inspiration

Under arches of shimmering light,
Ideas blossom, taking flight,
Each step we take, a story borne,
Inspiring hearts, a pact reborn.

Through corridors of vibrant dreams,
Passion flows in brilliant streams,
With every pulse, creativity grows,
In the depths, where the spirit knows.

Voices echo, gentle and clear,
Tales of courage, tales of fear,
We gather strength in this grand hall,
Through archways vast, we hear the call.

Halls of Whispers and Dreams

In halls adorned with silken threads,
Whispers linger, softly spread,
A tapestry of hopes and fears,
Echoing through the years.

Each step echoes with a sigh,
Memories held, they never die,
In shadows cast by candlelight,
Wisdom reigns when day meets night.

Here, the dreams and secrets blend,
Winds of time, they twist and bend,
In solitude, we find our voice,
In these halls, we make our choice.

Sanctum of the Muse

In the sacred space where artists dwell,
The muse whispers, casting a spell,
With every stroke, a story blooms,
In the sanctum where creativity looms.

The heart ignites with every sound,
In this haven, inspiration's found,
Threads of passion weave through air,
Beneath the gaze of the artist's stare.

Time stands still as visions rise,
Light and shadow, harmonize,
In the sacred dance of brush and pen,
The muse leads us time and again.

The Lighthouse of Visionary Hues

In twilight's glow, the beacon shines,
With colors bright, across the pines.
It guides the hearts, that seek the way,
Through stormy nights and break of day.

Each wave that crashes, sings a song,
Of dreams where lonely souls belong.
The lighthouse stands, a sentinel bold,
A keeper of tales, waiting to be told.

Upon the cliffs, with skies so vast,
The visions linger, shadows cast.
With every hue, a story spun,
In spiraled thoughts, where life's begun.

So let the light, like fireflies dance,
Illuminate the night, a chance.
For in each beam, a whisper clear,
Awakens hope, dispels the fear.

Celestial Gardens of the Imagination

In gardens vast, where stardust plays,
Dreams blossom bright in endless ways.
Each thought a flower, uniquely grown,
In cosmic soil where seeds are sown.

With petals soft as whispers shared,
Each color tells of hopes declared.
The moonlight weaves through branches high,
A tapestry against the sky.

Among the paths that twist and turn,
The heart ignites, with passions burn.
In every breeze, a gentle call,
Inviting souls to rise and fall.

So wander deep, where visions bloom,
In the celestial garden's room.
Where every dream, like stars alight,
Creates a world, both warm and bright.

The Nexus of New Narratives

In the realm where stories blend,
Tales of old and new transcend.
Voices rise, a chorus proud,
Whispers woven in the crowd.

Pages turning, hearts align,
Crafting dreams, we intertwine.
Each chapter sparks a fresh debate,
In this nexus, we create.

With every word, we stitch the seams,
Reviving long-forgotten dreams.
Metaphors dance, and truths unveil,
In unity, we shall prevail.

From shadows deep to light's embrace,
Narratives carve a sacred space.
Together we'll journey, share and explore,
At the nexus, we forever soar.

Canopies of Creative Revelations

Underneath a vibrant sky,
Ideas bloom and spirits fly.
Colors splash with every thought,
In this haven, dreams are caught.

Branches stretch, they intertwine,
Fostering visions, oh so divine.
Whispers of inspiration trail,
As imagination sets the sail.

Leaves of wisdom gently sway,
Guiding hearts along the way.
Each revelation, a bright spark,
In the canopy, dreams embark.

Together we'll gather, share the light,
Cultivating minds, day and night.
In this grove, our spirits thrive,
Under canopies, we come alive.

Foundations of Visionary Architecture

Bricks of thought, we lay them strong,
Crafting dreams, where we belong.
Designs that lift and spaces vast,
In this vision, futures cast.

Columns rise with purpose true,
Frameworks bend for me and you.
Blueprints drawn with careful hands,
In this architecture, hope expands.

Roofs of promise, skies above,
Towers built on dreams and love.
Each foundation stands with pride,
In visionary realms, we abide.

From whispers soft to echoes bold,
Stories of the brave retold.
Within these walls, we find our way,
In ideals, we shall not stray.

Ephemeral Echoes of Innovation

Fleeting moments whisper by,
In a flash, ideas fly high.
Echoes dance in fleeting air,
Innovation's spark ignites a flare.

Glimmers of change in twilight's hue,
Unfolding visions, fresh and new.
With each pulse, the future calls,
Ephemeral sights within these walls.

Threads of thought in time's embrace,
Chasing dreams we dare to face.
Every heartbeat tells a tale,
In the echoes, we shall prevail.

With daring hearts and minds afire,
We chase the light, we rise, aspire.
In the dance of now, we breathe,
In every echo, we believe.

Vaulted Ceilings of the Creative Heart

In a room where thoughts take flight,
Imaginations dance in the light.
Each whisper echoes, dreams unfurl,
A canvas painted in hopes that swirl.

With every brush and every pen,
New worlds emerge again and again.
The vaulted ceilings hold our art,
A testament to the creative heart.

Isles of Inspiration and Illusion

On distant shores where visions blend,
The island calls, a timeless friend.
Waves lap softly at dreams untold,
Each whisper carries tales of old.

Beneath the palm, illusions weave,
Inspiration flows, we dare believe.
These isles of light, a sacred place,
Where thoughts take shape, and ideas grace.

Chronicles in Sunlight and Shadow

In beams of gold, stories unfold,
In shadows deep, secrets are told.
Chronicles dance on the edge of night,
Illuminated in soft, gentle light.

Every moment, a fleeting spark,
In the glow of day, or the quiet dark.
History breathes in the balance we find,
Sunlight and shadow, intertwined.

Reveries Crafted in Silhouette

At twilight's kiss, dreams take their form,
Crafted in silhouette, they transform.
Figures waltz against the dusk,
In the embrace of night, we trust.

Each outline tells a tale so sweet,
Echoes dance, and hearts skip a beat.
Through the lens of dusk, we dare to roam,
In reveries crafted, we find our home.

Luminescent Labyrinths of Creation

In shadows weave the threads of light,
A dance of dreams that spark in night.
With whispers soft, the pathways call,
Through winding turns, we rise and fall.

Each step a brush, each thought a hue,
Colors blend, creating new.
In this maze where wonders gleam,
We find ourselves within the dream.

Shrines of the Soul's Craft

In silence grow the seeds of grace,
Within the heart, a sacred space.
With hands like clay, we shape our fate,
In these shrines, we liberate.

Crafting stories, building souls,
Filling voids, making whole.
With each creation, voices rise,
In every form, the spirit flies.

Pillars of Passion and Purpose

On steadfast ground, our dreams take root,
In the heart's forge, we find the truth.
With fire and fervor, we stand tall,
These pillars hold us through it all.

With every choice, our paths align,
In the dance of life, we intertwine.
Purpose guides through the darkest nights,
Passions born as the soul ignites.

The Echo Chamber of Ideas

In the chamber, thoughts resound,
Voices echo, wisdom found.
Each idea a spark, a flare,
Together creating visions rare.

Through twists of mind, we navigate,
In this space, we elevate.
Reflections deep, the wisdom grows,
From each exchange, a new path shows.

The Altar of Expression

Words like whispers float in air,
Painted dreams with colors rare.
Voices rise, a sacred chant,
In the heart, emotions slant.

Canvas stretches, stories told,
Every stroke a chance to hold.
Fingers trace the lines of fate,
In this space, we dare create.

Shadows dance and sunlight plays,
In the mind, a vibrant maze.
Each creation breathes, alive,
Here where thoughts and spirits thrive.

Vaults of Visionary Spirit

In the depths of silent night,
Ideas soar, ablaze with light.
Visions float on cosmic streams,
Brought to life from waking dreams.

Every brushstroke, truth revealed,
In these vaults, our fates are sealed.
Imagination's gentle guide,
Within us all, our spirits bide.

As colors merge and shapes collide,
In the chaos, we confide.
From the shadows, brilliance bursts,
In the silence, art immerses.

Sanctified Spaces of Art

Here in corners softly lit,
Creativity dares to sit.
Every glance can spark a flame,
In each heart, art calls a name.

Whispers of the past reside,
In this space, we stand with pride.
Echoes of a thousand hands,
In these walls, the spirit stands.

Brushes dance to silent songs,
Where the soul of wonder throngs.
In this sanctuary bright,
Art's embrace ignites the night.

Ruins Reborn in Color

Once was loss, now vibrant hues,
From the dust, we shape our views.
Crumbled edges, stories weave,
In decay, we learn to believe.

Brick by brick, a tale restored,
Through the pain, our spirits soared.
Colors splash on ancient stone,
In rebirth, we feel at home.

Echoes of the past abide,
As the canvas is our guide.
From the ruins, beauty springs,
In the change, the heart still sings.

Sanctuary of Shattered Norms

In a world where rules unwind,
Dreamers gather, hearts aligned.
With colors bright and voices loud,
They weave their tales, a vibrant crowd.

Shattered norms, they rise and soar,
Breaking silence, seeking more.
In this haven, all belong,
Together we form a sacred song.

Beneath the stars, they find their place,
In each other's eyes, a warm embrace.
Embracing truth, they stand as one,
In the sanctuary, shadows run.

So let the laughter pierce the night,
As hopes ignite with brilliant light.
In this realm, where visions bloom,
Shattered norms break every gloom.

Spheres of Artistic Abundance

In circles bright, the artists play,
Creating worlds, in bright array.
With every stroke, a tale unfolds,
Within the spheres, a magic holds.

In vibrant hues, their souls ignite,
Crafting dreams in pure delight.
Sculpted forms, their visions soar,
In this abundance, they seek more.

Whispers flow through canvas air,
Each artist's heart, laid bare.
Threads of passion, tightly spun,
In every piece, a journey begun.

Together, they share the flame,
In these spheres, no two the same.
Bound by love for art so true,
Across the canvas, skies of blue.

Enclaves of Whimsy and Wonder

In hidden nooks where dreamers dwell,
Whimsy and wonder weave their spell.
Through laughter light and stories gleam,
They float along like a vivid dream.

With drawings bold and voices bright,
They dance through days and twinkling nights.
Each enclave holds a secret key,
Unlocking hearts to set them free.

Magic spins in every glance,
Inviting souls to join the dance.
With open arms and open minds,
In wondrous realms, connection finds.

So wander deep where shadows play,
In enclaves bright where spirits sway.
Together in surreal delight,
Sparkling eyes reflect the light.

Spirals of Thoughtful Tension

In spirals deep, emotions twist,
Thoughtful moments, too hard to miss.
Echoes of doubt, truths intertwine,
Within each soul, a fragile line.

Balancing dreams on shifting ground,
In whispered fears, answers are found.
A dance of shadows, light and dark,
Each heartbeat sings, igniting spark.

Through winding paths, their thoughts collide,
In every corner, secrets hide.
Truth and beauty, hand in hand,
In thoughtful tension, they take a stand.

With careful steps, they seek the way,
In spirals turning, night and day.
For in this space, they find their voice,
Embracing struggle, they rejoice.

Porticos of the Poetic Mind

In shadows cast by ink-stained dreams,
Whispers of the heart take flight,
Through passages of thought they gleam,
In silence blooms the spark of light.

Fragments of a vibrant hue,
Dance upon the canvas bare,
Converging worlds, both old and new,
Where poets linger unaware.

Each sigh a verse, each glance a word,
Resonating truths they find,
In melodies that once were heard,
Awakening the tautly wound mind.

Underneath the starlit dome,
Reflections merge, collide, entwine,
Within this space, we feel at home,
Porticos of the poetic mind.

Odes Beyond Physical Boundaries

Fleeting echoes of the soul,
Stretch beyond the limits brief,
In whispered tales, we seek the whole,
Creating realms beyond belief.

Bridges formed with lines of grace,
Linking hearts across the sky,
In every note, a sacred space,
Where dreams take flight, learn how to fly.

Through dimensions unforeseen,
We sail on verses, rise and bend,
Odes that weave what might have been,
Connecting us, time cannot end.

In infinity's embrace we find,
Resonant truths, both wide and deep,
Beyond the limits of mankind,
Odes beyond physical boundaries keep.

Elysian Fields of Innovation

In gardens full of vibrant thought,
Where ideas sprout and glow,
Each moment traded, lessons taught,
In fertile ground where visions grow.

With gentle winds the whispers shift,
Sowing seeds of dreams anew,
In unity, our spirits lift,
Creating paths where few once flew.

Imagination, a thriving river,
Carving valleys of the mind,
In every turn, a spark delivered,
Elysian fields, where futures find.

We'll wander through this sacred space,
Where creativity blooms in grace,
Innovation's light starts to trace,
Elysian fields of innovation's embrace.

The Refuge of Unbounded Creativity

Within the realm of endless dreams,
Where thoughts collide and merge with light,
Imagination flows in streams,
Creating worlds beyond our sight.

A sanctuary for the soul,
In shadows cast by fervent muse,
Here wanderers gather, spirits whole,
In colors bright, they choose to fuse.

With every brush, with every pen,
We sculpt the stories yet untold,
In the refuge of light again,
Where every heart can dare be bold.

A tapestry of voices rise,
In harmony, our truths unite,
A haven found beneath the skies,
The refuge of unbounded creativity's light.

Grounds for the Growth of Ideas

In the quiet soil of thought,
Seeds of dreams are gently sown.
With patience, water, and love,
New visions begin to bloom.

Sunlight breaks the darkened night,
Nurturing the fragile sprouts.
Each idea reaches for the sky,
In whispers, a voice shouts.

Roots entwine in rich embrace,
Holding fast to fertile ground.
From whispers to a vivid place,
Where innovation can be found.

Through seasons, winds, and rains,
The garden of thoughts expands.
With tender care and gentle hands,
A symphony of change remains.

Sculpted Dreams in Celestial Light

Underneath the boundless sky,
Dreams are carved from starlit air.
Each contour a silent sigh,
Whispered hopes beyond compare.

In the glow of moonlit beams,
Visions dance and take their flight.
Chiseled by the hands of dreams,
Formed anew in sacred light.

A canvas of the cosmic seas,
Where the heart finds its refrain.
With each brushstroke, a gentle breeze,
Painting wonders free from pain.

Through the nebulae and gleam,
Imagination soars as free.
In the silence, we find our theme,
Sculpted souls in harmony.

Echoes of the Unseen Artistry

In shadows where no one goes,
Artistry breathes soft and low.
Hidden echoes, subtle flows,
In silence, creativity grows.

Each brushstroke a quiet tale,
Crafted by the midnight muse.
In the stillness, the heart prevails,
With colors the world can choose.

Fragments of a dream unwind,
Whispers carried through the night.
Every thought is intertwined,
With the beauty of pure light.

As shadows dance their sacred waltz,
The unseen becomes a song.
In the quiet, the heart exalts,
Celebrating all along.

The Gallery of Untamed Thoughts

Walls adorned with vibrant dreams,
Each canvas tells a new refrain.
In this space, nothing is as it seems,
Every brushstroke a loving chain.

Echoes of laughter fill the air,
While shadows play with hidden grace.
Fragments of souls laid bare,
In this wild, uncharted place.

Through colors bold and lines untamed,
Thoughts collide in joyous dance.
None are ever quite the same,
In this ever-shifting trance.

From chaos springs a vibrant view,
Where imagination knows no bounds.
In this gallery, hearts break through,
In the silence, true art resounds.

The Forge of Infinite Insights

In the heart of the flame, ideas ignite,
Crafted by hands that know no night.
Wisdom flows through molten streams,
Sculpting reality from the fabric of dreams.

Chisels strike with purpose clear,
Each mark a thought that draws us near.
Patterns emerge from the heat's embrace,
Transforming chaos into grace.

Minds converge like rivers wide,
In the forge, our truths abide.
Through tempered steel and fervent fire,
We shape a world that lifts us higher.

Each creation a story told,
In the heat of passion, brave and bold.
Infinite insights rise and soar,
From the depths of the forge, we explore.

Sanctums Cloaked in Colors

Hidden realms where shadows play,
Sanctums bloom in vibrant display.
Crimson whispers, azure sighs,
Each hue a secret, cloaked in lies.

Vines entwine with golden light,
Crafting tapestries, day and night.
In every corner, colors blend,
Welcoming hearts that dare to transcend.

Pillars of green, soft and deep,
Guard the dreams that we wish to keep.
Through painted paths, the spirit dances,
In this haven, life enhances.

Emerging hues ignite the soul,
A sanctuary that makes us whole.
In cloaked colors, we find our song,
In this sanctum, we all belong.

Aetherial Spaces of Expression

Vast expanse where thoughts take flight,
Aetherial whispers in the night.
Voices rise like gentle streams,
Flowing into the realm of dreams.

In silence, echoes craft their tale,
Each breath a color, soft and pale.
Words weave together, strong and fine,
Creating bridges where spirits align.

Floating high on wings of thought,
Ideas glimmer where time is caught.
In these spaces, we boldly roam,
Finding in expression, a sacred home.

Unbounded realms, where visions grow,
In aetherial light, they freely flow.
Through the cosmos of the mind,
Endless wonders, we seek and find.

Visions Nestled within Stone Shadows

In stone shadows, visions hide,
Whispers of the past collide.
Each crevice holds a tale untold,
Memories wrapped in silence cold.

Moss carpets paths that once were bright,
Guarding the secrets of day and night.
Carved in rock, our dreams await,
Awakening spirits that resonate.

Flickering flames cast dancing light,
Illuminating shadows with gentle might.
Through fissures deep, the future gleams,
In stone shadows, we weave our dreams.

Nestled within, a vibrant spark,
Illuminates the world so dark.
In stillness, visions softly grow,
In the home of shadows, we come to know.

The Courtyards of Creation

In gardens where the wild things play,
Ideas bloom in vibrant sway.
Whispers of dreams take flight anew,
Crafting worlds with shades of hue.

Each stone laid tells a tale profound,
Echoes of genius all around.
Beneath the arching sky so wide,
In these courtyards, hopes abide.

With every brush, a vision born,
From dusk till the light of dawn.
Creation dances, light and free,
In this sacred space, we see.

So wander through this hallowed place,
Embrace each moment, every trace.
For in the heart of art's embrace,
We find our truth, our boundless space.

Stained Glass of Emotions

Colors fracture, sunlight bends,
In patterns where the heart transcends.
Each shard a feeling, bright and bold,
Stories of love and pain retold.

When shadows mingle with the light,
Fragments sparkle, warm and bright.
Cascading hues on walls of grace,
Reflections that the soul can trace.

In moments caught, the joy, the ache,
A tapestry of what we make.
Through every feeling, sharp or sweet,
We find the beauty in defeat.

Let the light grant us its gleam,
In this mosaic, we can dream.
For through the glass, we surely see,
The hues of life, our history.

The Resonance of Purpose

In silent chambers where echoes arise,
A symphony born from the heart's sighs.
Whispers of why guide the way,
As dreams and desires gently sway.

With every step, a beat, a call,
Building bridges, preventing the fall.
A rhythm found in strife and peace,
In purpose, our striving never cease.

The notes we play, both soft and loud,
A tapestry woven, vibrant, proud.
In every rise and every fall,
The resonance unites us all.

So let the sound of life unfold,
Each resonant purpose, bright and bold.
Together we stand, hand in hand,
In harmony, we find our land.

Atriums of Originality

In open spaces, fresh and bright,
Ideas flutter, taking flight.
Whirls of thought, like leaves in breeze,
In every corner, creativity frees.

With sunlight spilling through the panes,
Singular visions break the chains.
In these atriums where we explore,
The essence of what we adore.

Innovation thrives in every nook,
Each glance reveals a storybook.
Through shards of brilliance, we awake,
To carve our mark, no fear, no fake.

So gather here, let's dare to share,
In this sanctuary, free from care.
For originality is our song,
A melody where we all belong.

The Asylum for Artistic Souls

In shadows deep where colors dance,
A haven waits for chance and chance.
With canvases of dreams untold,
Their visions bright, their spirits bold.

The echoes of the silent muse,
In a room where none refuse.
Each brushstroke whispers to the night,
A symphony of pure delight.

With laughter ringing through the halls,
Where every heartbeat softly calls.
In this retreat, the curious blend,
Of art and life where dreams ascend.

So gather close, the wayward hearts,
In this abode where passion starts.
For every soul that dares to soar,
The asylum waits, forevermore.

Bridges Across the Void of Normalcy

In the stillness, whispers rise,
Crafting paths 'neath painted skies.
With each step, the world expands,
Embracing dreams within our hands.

Connect the dots from heart to mind,
Where all the lost hopes are redefined.
With courage sewn in threads of light,
To bridge the gap from dark to bright.

The norm may tremble at the sight,
Of those who dare ignite the night.
With bridges built from love and grace,
Together we shall find our place.

So take a breath, unlace your fears,
Cross the chasm, dry your tears.
For in this quest of self-discovery,
We find our truth, our history.

Euphoria in a Whispered Creation

In gentle strokes, the magic grows,
A dance of words that softly flows.
With every syllable a spark,
Igniting dreams within the dark.

The silence speaks in vibrant hues,
As visions form in shades of blues.
Creation whispers tenderly,
Awakening what's meant to be.

In whispered breaths, emotions spill,
A canvas alive with fervent will.
Euphoria entwined with each line,
In this creation, we align.

So let your heart in tempo sway,
Express the joys of light and play.
For in this realm where voices gleam,
Awaken life within the dream.

The Sacred Rite of Originality

In the sacred space of truth defined,
We seek the voice that's most aligned.
Each thought a treasure, raw and rare,
In silence, we breathe life with care.

The craft bestowed by hands unique,
A melody in every peak.
With every stroke, we carve our mark,
Originality ignites the spark.

The rite unfolds with every choice,
To hear our frequency, our voice.
With courage bold, we tread our way,
In a world that longs for us to stay.

So celebrate the path we tread,
With passion burning, dreams widespread.
For in the heart of what is true,
The sacred rite shines, ever new.

Pillars of Infinite Thought

In quiet corners, wisdom stands,
Rooted deep in ancient lands.
Ideas bloom like flowers bright,
With every mind, a spark of light.

Echoing through the halls of time,
Thoughts expand, a silent rhyme.
Carved in stone, yet soft as air,
In every heart, a dream laid bare.

Voices whisper, secrets shared,
On these paths, we've all prepared.
A journey vast, through realms unseen,
Each pillar strong, each moment keen.

Woven threads of every tale,
In unity, we shall not fail.
Through infinite thought, we rise above,
Embraced by hope, defined by love.

Echoes of Artisan Souls

Hands that craft with tender grace,
Shaping dreams, an artful space.
From clay and wood, the stories flow,
In every piece, a heart aglow.

Whispers linger in the air,
Echoes of the soul laid bare.
Each creation tells its tale,
Of joy, of struggle, of love's prevail.

Colors dance, and shadows blend,
An artisan's touch, a lifelong friend.
With every stroke, a vision soars,
In every heart, a craft restores.

Gathered here, we celebrate,
Artisan souls, we resonate.
With hands united, voices strong,
In echoes, we find where we belong.

Tapestries of Innovation

Threads of thought, a vibrant weave,
In every shade, the dreams conceive.
Ideas spun on looms of fate,
In artistry, we navigate.

From whispers to a mighty roar,
Innovation opens every door.
Patterns shifting, bold and bright,
In the fabric of the night.

Minds entwined in a dance so grand,
Creating futures with steady hand.
Every stitch a mark of pride,
In this tapestry, we confide.

United visions, we will soar,
In the embrace of evermore.
With threads of hope, we intertwine,
Crafting wonders, by design.

Chambers of Light and Shadow

In chambers vast, where whispers play,
Light and shadow intertwine their sway.
A dance of contrast, bold and rare,
Revealing truths that dwell in air.

Silent echoes haunt the night,
In dim-lit corners, flickers bright.
Every shadow holds a story,
In darkness too, we find our glory.

Wisdom pulses in the gloom,
In haze, we find a fragrant bloom.
Yet light reveals the paths we tread,
In balance found, we forge ahead.

Together in this endless flow,
We learn to cherish both high and low.
In chambers of our heart's embrace,
We are the light, we are the space.

Woven Narratives in the Sky

Clouds drift softly, stories untold,
Under twilight, mysteries unfold.
Stars are whispers, secrets they share,
Painting dreams in the night air.

Moonbeams dance on the ocean's face,
Guiding hearts to a tranquil place.
Each shimmer a tale, bright and clear,
Echoes of laughter, drawing near.

In the tapestry, colors entwine,
Drawing paths through the night's design.
Weaving moments, love's gentle sigh,
In the fabric of the endless sky.

Guardians of Enlightened Browsing

In pixels and codes, wisdom flows bright,
Guardians watch in the digital light.
Each search a journey, seeking the true,
Connecting minds, both old and new.

A click in the dark, a spark ignites,
Opening doors to the world's insights.
Navigating streams of thought and care,
With each discovery, wisdom to share.

Threads of knowledge, woven with grace,
In the vast expanse, we find our place.
Guardians guide us, steering the quest,
Through the labyrinth, we are blessed.

Wells of Imaginative Thought

Within our minds, deep wells reside,
Where creativity and dreams abide.
Sip from the waters, let visions bloom,
Illuminate shadows, dispel the gloom.

Each drop of insight, a spark of fire,
Fueling the dreams that ever inspire.
Diving deeper, where ideas flow,
In the quiet moments, secrets grow.

Wells of wonder, endless and deep,
Harvesting thoughts that never sleep.
With every splash, a new path is drawn,
Imagination wakes with the dawn.

Aurora Above the Realm of Dreamers

Dancing lights in the midnight sky,
Auroras whisper to those who fly.
Dreamers gather where colors beam,
Chasing visions, alive in the dream.

Flickering hues paint the dark night,
Stirring souls with a soft, bright light.
Each wave of brilliance, a beckoning call,
Inviting all to the dance of the thrall.

Let aspirations rise with the glow,
As the heart's desires begin to flow.
Above the realm where dreamers roam,
Aurora sings, leading them home.

The Labyrinth of Luminous Dreams

In the maze of night, we wander,
Chasing glimmers, soft and bright.
Each turn a place to ponder,
A dance of shadows, of light.

Whispers call from hidden paths,
Breezes carry tales untold.
In this world, our heartbeats laugh,
Dreams unfold like threads of gold.

Twisting ways, a secret art,
Woven through our restless mind.
Lost and found, we play our part,
In the solace we must find.

With every step, a choice we make,
Into the depths of the unknown.
In this labyrinth, we awake,
To find the seeds we've sown.

Wonders within the Imaginative Walls

Within these walls, the colors breathe,
Whispers of wishes linger here.
Each corner holds a tale to weave,
Stories born from joy and fear.

Minds ignite with vivid flight,
Flights of fancy, wild and free.
In shadows cast, we find the light,
Imagination's tapestry.

Frescoes dance on ancient stone,
Dreams exploding, bright and bold.
In this space, we are not alone,
Hearts and minds, a world of gold.

Glimmers spark in every thought,
Painting visions fierce and grand.
In this realm, our souls are caught,
Crafting life with gentle hands.

Lanterns of Belief and Brilliance

In the night, bright lanterns gleam,
Each flicker tells a tale anew.
Their glow ignites the darkest dream,
A guiding light, a path to view.

Stars align with whispered grace,
Hold your fears in gentle light.
In this dance, we find our place,
Belief ignites within the night.

Reflections of what's yet to come,
Hope rides high on wings of chance.
In the silence, steady drum,
Brilliance blooms in every glance.

So lift your lantern, let it shine,
Through the shadows, hold it near.
In this journey, you'll find mine,
Together, we'll conquer fear.

Structures Built on Hope

Upon the ground where dreams arise,
We build our structures, brick by brick.
In every heart, a wish complies,
Hope stands tall, the strongest stick.

Foundations laid with purpose true,
Courage crafted from our past.
With every stone, we break on through,
A legacy designed to last.

High above, the sky unwinds,
Each beam a testament of will.
In our hands, the future binds,
With every heartbeat, dreams fulfill.

So let us raise our towers high,
Over valleys of despair.
On wings of hope, we learn to fly,
In unity, we find our care.

The Mosaic of Collective Wonder

In colors bright, we weave our dreams,
A dance of thoughts, like flowing streams.
Together we blend our hopes and fears,
Creating a tapestry through the years.

Laughter and whispers, both intertwine,
Our stories shared, a sacred design.
With every piece a story told,
A mosaic rich, in hues of gold.

Voices rising, like birds in flight,
Each note a spark, igniting the night.
In unity, we find our grace,
A collective wonder, a shared embrace.

As we gather under the starlit sky,
Together we reach, together we fly.
Each thread a bond, a tale we share,
In the mosaic of life, we find our care.

Labyrinths of the Mind's Eye

Winding paths of thought unfold,
In shadows cast, our stories told.
Through twists and turns, we seek the light,
In the labyrinth's depths, we find our sight.

Images flicker, memories dance,
In echoes of silence, we take our chance.
Dreams and fears, both intertwine,
In the corridors where our minds align.

Every choice a path to tread,
In the maze of thoughts that swirl in red.
Finding clarity through what we feel,
In these labyrinths, our souls reveal.

As we navigate the twists of fate,
With courage found, we shall create.
In the mind's embrace, we will explore,
The beauty hidden in every door.

Echoing Canvases of the Heart

Brush strokes bold, colors entwined,
On canvases vast, our spirits aligned.
Each heartbeat echoes, a vibrant hue,
In the art of love, we find what's true.

Whispers of longing, painted with care,
In layers thick, we lay ourselves bare.
With every touch, a story unfolds,
An echoing canvas of tales untold.

Shadows dance beneath the light,
In every corner, love takes flight.
A masterpiece forged in moments shared,\nOur hearts
reflect the dreams we dared.

As we laugh, as we cry,
In strokes of joy, our spirits fly.
On this canvas, we'll leave our mark,
In the gallery of life, bright and stark.

Spires of Celestial Ideas

Reaching high toward the endless sky,
Spires of thoughts that soar and fly.
In the cradle of stars, our visions bloom,
Illuminating paths through the darkened room.

Ideas like comets streaking past,
In the cosmos of dreams, they hold steadfast.
With every spark, a universe born,
In the light of wisdom, we are reborn.

Together we build, with hearts as one,
In the realm of science, we have just begun.
Each mind a beacon, guiding the way,
In spires of thought, we seize the day.

As we climb towards the shining night,
Inspiration flows, a boundless flight.
In the heights of dreams, we find our place,
In celestial ideas, we weave our grace.

Pillars of Artistic Expression

Brush strokes dance on canvas bare,
Colors clash with vivid flair.
Melodies soar through air so light,
Crafting dreams in day and night.

Words entwine in poetic form,
Voices rise, creativity's warm.
Sculptors shape with patient hands,
Art, the language that understands.

Photographs capture fleeting time,
Moments frozen in rhythm and rhyme.
Each creation, a sacred rite,
Pillars strong, standing in light.

In galleries where silence breathes,
The heart finds peace, the spirit weaves.
In every piece, a story told,
Art's embrace, both fierce and bold.

Tapestries of Thought and Fantasy

Threads of imagination intertwine,
Weaving worlds where dreams align.
Fables told in vibrant hues,
Magic dances, whispers muse.

In shadows deep, the stories play,
Illuminated by thoughts that sway.
Every tale, a portal bright,
Guides us through the endless night.

In the realm of fantasy's grip,
Many a heart begins to skip.
Tapestry rich, with lore combined,
Unveiling secrets of the mind.

Each stitch a journey, a voice to share,
Details spun with loving care.
In this fabric, life expands,
Tapestries woven by gentle hands.

Echoes in the Halls of Invention

Echoes bounce off ancient walls,
Whispers of genius in grand halls.
Inventions forged in fierce embrace,
Innovation leaves its trace.

Ideas clash in brilliant light,
Minds converge to take their flight.
Each creation, a legacy,
Marking time, a tapestry.

Fires of thought flicker and flare,
Invention dances on the air.
From simple tools to wondrous sights,
The spark of change ignites the nights.

History's echo, loud and clear,
In every vision, we draw near.
The halls resound with dreams that grow,
Inventive minds, the seeds we sow.

Sanctified Spaces of Inspiration

In quiet corners where muses dwell,
Sanctified spaces, hearts can tell.
Nature's whispers, soft and low,
In these realms, creativity flows.

Sunlight filters through leafy green,
Awakens thoughts, vibrant and keen.
With every breath, ideas ignite,
In sacred peace, the world feels right.

Journals filled with hope and dreams,
Inspiration's touch, like gentle streams.
Every word, a step so bold,
Sanctified spaces, stories unfold.

Where silence reigns and hearts unite,
Creativity blooms, bathed in light.
In these hallowed grounds, we find,
Sanctuary for the restless mind.

Reverberations of a Silent Muse

In shadows deep, she whispers soft,
A melody not heard aloft.
Through silent halls, her echoes roam,
Awakening hearts, calling them home.

With gentle hands, she molds the air,
Crafting dreams beyond compare.
Each stroke a sigh, a fleeting glance,
In her embrace, we find our chance.

The canvas waits, a waiting soul,
Colors blend, creating whole.
Through muted tones, her voice takes flight,
Guiding us into the light.

In reverberations, truths unfold,
Stories of the brave and bold.
Forever bound by her sweet grace,
We dance together, face to face.

The Odyssey of Artistic Souls

Upon the waves, the brushes sail,
Chasing hues in a boundless trail.
With every stroke, they navigate,
Crafting worlds through love and fate.

Through stormy nights and tranquil dawns,
Inspiration bursts like the morning fawns.
From visions deep to skies so wide,
Artistic souls become the tide.

On parchment paths, their dreams entwine,
With sparkling thoughts that brightly shine.
In every heart, a fire glows,
The odyssey of art bestows.

Through timeless quests, old and new,
We find a spark in every hue.
An endless journey, forever bold,
United in stories yet untold.

Crypts of Hidden Inspiration

In ancient crypts, where silence reigns,
Whispers weave through dusty grains.
From shadows deep, a spark may rise,
In hidden realms where beauty lies.

Each corner holds a tale untold,
Of fractured dreams and hearts of gold.
In cues of twilight, visions flare,
Unraveled secrets linger in the air.

Among the ruins, echoes play,
Inviting artists to stay and sway.
With open minds, they dare to seek,
The hidden muse, unique and meek.

Through crypts of time, a fire ignites,
Inspiring souls to reach new heights.
So venture forth, embrace the call,
In hidden depths, we find it all.

Towers of Untold Stories

In towers high, where dreams reside,
The tales of old strengthen with pride.
Each brick a whisper, each stone a scream,
Building a world from fractured dreams.

Through winding paths, our hearts take flight,
With every chapter, revealing light.
From ancient scripts, our spirits soar,
Towers rise with tales of yore.

In every room, a vibe we feel,
Stories flow like spinning wheels.
Characters dance, both fierce and bold,
Their lives entwined in threads of gold.

As we ascend through endless lore,
The towers beckon us for more.
In this domain of dreams and plight,
Untold stories ignite the night.

Embers of Forgotten Visions

In twilight's glow, lost dreams ignite,
Flickering shadows, fading light.
Silent echoes of what once was,
Heartbeats linger, pause and cause.

Whispers of hope, yearning in flames,
Memories dance, forgetting names.
Through ashes grey, the spark reveals,
The warmth of time, the depth of feels.

In lonely nights, we search the skies,
For glimpses of love in unseen ties.
Embers fade, but hearts remain,
A glow of truth within the pain.

Each flicker whispers, "Don't let go,"
For in the dark, our feelings grow.
As visions blur, we still believe,
In embers bright, we find reprieve.

Whispers Beneath Sacred Arches

Beneath the arches, whispers flow,
Secrets held where shadows glow.
Timeworn stones, stories they share,
In silence deep, they breathe the air.

The gentle sigh of breeze and tree,
Holds sacred tales, just you and me.
We walk through halls where echoes dwell,
In every corner, a wishful spell.

Sunlight dapples on ancient ground,
In stillness found, the lost is found.
Each footstep pressed speaks to the heart,
In sacred space, we play our part.

With every breath, the past collides,
In whispered tones, our spirit guides.
Under the arches, we remain,
Forever held in love's refrain.

Infinity in the Stone Canvas

In the heart of stone, time unfolds,
Shapes and patterns, whispers told.
Chiseled dreams by hands of old,
A canvas vast, with stories bold.

Each crevice holds a piece of fate,
Infinity waits, it won't hesitate.
Veins of quartz, veins of time,
In stillness, life learns to climb.

Silent witnesses through the years,
Bridging moments, joys and tears.
Echoes linger, never cease,
In stone, we find our inner peace.

Carved reminders of all we've been,
Reflections flash, our lives to glean.
In every grain, a journey spins,
Infinity waits as life begins.

Fountains of Aesthetic Reverie

In garden dreams where waters play,
Fountains bloom in soft ballet.
Each drop a note in nature's song,
A dance of light where hearts belong.

Ripples weave through verdant grass,
Time slows down as moments pass.
Reflections shimmer, colors bright,
In aesthetic splendor, pure delight.

Petals fall like whispered dreams,
Transforming streams with silver beams.
The air is thick with fragrant bliss,
In every splash, a lover's kiss.

Beneath the skies, we find our way,
In fountain's grace, we choose to stay.
Where beauty flows, and dreams arise,
Life's reverie, beneath the skies.

Alchemical Passages of the Mind

In shadows deep, the thoughts unfold,
Alchemy of dreams, a tale retold.
Whispers of wisdom, lost in time,
Transforming moments, pure and sublime.

Through corridors where visions flow,
An elixir brewed from what we know.
Mind's alchemy, a dance in space,
Crafting perception, leaving a trace.

Each thought a spark, igniting the night,
Turning the simple into pure light.
A journey within, where wonders blend,
Alchemical pathways never end.

In silence, the secrets softly weave,
Layers of meaning, what we perceive.
Unlocking the door to the sacred art,
Alchemy lives in the beating heart.

A Convergence of Inspirations

In the quiet hum of twilight's glow,
Ideas gather, in whispers they flow.
Minds entwined, a tapestry spins,
A convergence of thoughts, where all begins.

From visions bright, like stars they spring,
Each spark ignites, and the heart takes wing.
In shared silence, creation ignites,
Harmonies born on the canvas of nights.

Crossroads of dreams, where fates interlace,
Bridges of passion, each step a grace.
Impressions linger, like dew on the grass,
Inspiration thrives, and moments amass.

A symphony played on the strings of the soul,
Melodies rich, making the spirit whole.
In this space, we find our way,
A convergence of wonders, come what may.

Ethereal Structures of the Heart and Mind

In realms unseen, where shadows play,
Ethereal towers rise, holding sway.
Thoughts like whispers, dance in the air,
Structures of beauty, light and rare.

Craftsmanship of emotion, so divine,
Foundations of love in each design.
Bridges built from laughter and sighs,
Ethereal forms that reach for the skies.

With every heartbeat, a rhythm flows,
Mapping the journey, where the spirit goes.
Layers of feeling, gently align,
Crafting a world that's truly divine.

In twilight's embrace, we find our peace,
Ethereal structures that never cease.
Hearts and minds, in harmony blend,
In this sacred space, where dreams transcend.

The Repository of Untold Genius

In the depths of silence, wisdom resides,
A repository vast, where secrets abide.
Untold genius, whispers of old,
Treasures of insight waiting to unfold.

Like ancient tomes with pages worn,
Ideas bloom, like flowers, reborn.
Each thought a gem, precious and rare,
Hiding in places, seldom laid bare.

In each heartbeat, a story lives,
Echoes of brilliance, the soul forgives.
Unlocking the vaults, we seek to explore,
The repository of dreams, forevermore.

In the minds we gather, and hearts we share,
Untold genius, woven with care.
So let us journey into the unknown,
Where wisdom unfolds, and seeds are sown.

The Treasury of Found Dreams

In shadows deep, where whispers dwell,
The treasure lies, all tales to tell.
A golden chest of hopes once lost,
Held tightly, with love, no matter the cost.

Each dream a gem, a fleeting light,
Shimmering softly in the night.
They call to souls, both brave and meek,
In hearts awakened, they softly speak.

With open hands, we gather near,
To cherish dreams we hold so dear.
In silence, we let visions soar,
Each one a key to a hidden door.

So come, dear friend, and take your place,
Embrace the magic, meet each grace.
In this treasury, we find our theme,
Together we weave the fabric of dream.

Sanctuaries of Imagination

Beneath the boughs, where thoughts can roam,
Imagination carves a secret home.
A sanctuary wrapped in gentle light,
Where fears dissolve, and spirits take flight.

With colors bright, the palette's wide,
In every heart, a place to hide.
Here, dreams blend like the evening hues,
In whispered songs, our hearts enthuse.

Time stands still, as stories play,
In corners where the wild dreams sway.
With every heartbeat, visions grow,
In sacred spaces, let courage flow.

So wander far, and dare to see,
The endless realms of possibility.
In sanctuaries of our design,
Imagination blooms, a gift divine.

Architectural Dreams in Verses

In blueprints drawn on starlit skies,
We craft our visions, let them rise.
Each word a brick, each thought a beam,
Constructing worlds from our shared dream.

A tower built from whispered hopes,
Rising high, as each spirit copes.
In arches wide, our laughter rings,
Through open doors, the joy it brings.

Foundations set in timeless ground,
With every page, new layers found.
The lines of fate, we deftly trace,
In architectural dreams, our embrace.

So sketch your heart, and carve your name,
In verses echoing love's pure flame.
Together we build, both strong and free,
A structure of dreams, for all to see.

The Altar of Enlightenment

In quiet spaces, shadows blend,
The altar stands, where journeys end.
With candles lit, the mind takes flight,
In search of wisdom, pure and bright.

Each thought a offering, laid with care,
On sacred grounds, we pause and stare.
With open hearts, the truth we seek,
In gentle whispers, the soul can speak.

Guided by the stars above,
In every moment, we find pure love.
The altar glows, an inner flame,
Where questions echo, never the same.

So gather close, and heed the call,
In enlightenment, we rise, we fall.
With every breath, a lesson learned,
At the altar of truth, our hearts are turned.

The Shrine of Wonderment

In twilight's glow, the shadows dance,
Where dreams awake, and hopes advance.
A whisper stirs the silent air,
A hidden world beyond compare.

With gentle light, the secrets gleam,
Each corner holds a silent dream.
In every heart, a tale to weave,
A tapestry of what we believe.

The echoes of the past reside,
In every breath, in every stride.
The shrine calls forth with open arms,
Inviting souls to its quiet charms.

Among the stars, the wonders shine,
In the sacred space, all hearts align.
Together in this sacred place,
We find our truth, our common grace.

Portals to the Untold

Beneath the veil of night's embrace,
Lies a gateway to a boundless space.
Through whispers soft, the echoes lead,
To stories yet to plant their seed.

Each doorway framed with mystic light,
Invites the brave to take the flight.
Beyond the known, where shadows play,
The untold tales await the day.

Step forth with courage, shed the fear,
In every heart, the truth is near.
With open minds, the wonders swell,
In portals vast, we break the spell.

Through cosmic paths, we wander free,
With every step, a new decree.
The mysteries of life unfold,
In the chambers of the untold.

Banners of Artistic Revolt

In splashes bold, the colors clash,
Where whispers of rebellion flash.
With every stroke, a message clear,
The banners rise, igniting cheer.

Voices loud, with hearts ablaze,
In vibrant hues, we set the gaze.
The canvas breathes with life anew,
A revolution painted true.

Minds unchained, we dare to dream,
A work of art, a daring theme.
From ashes rise, the fearless wave,
With banners high, we boldly pave.

Each brush a weapon, each note a cry,
In this revolt, we reach the sky.
The art we make, a legacy,
Of freedom's song, our symphony.

The Crypt of Uncharted Thoughts

In shadows deep, where silence reigns,
Lie whispers locked in hidden chains.
The crypt of dreams, a sacred tomb,
Where echoes linger, flowers bloom.

With every breath, a secret sigh,
A garden grown where thoughts can fly.
In rifled depths, the treasure lies,
Unraveled truths and hidden skies.

Step lightly on this hallowed ground,
In crypts of thought, the lost are found.
With gentle hands, we lift the veil,
And through the dark, our minds set sail.

In every corner, wisdom glows,
As seeds of wonder softly grow.
The crypt once closed, now open wide,
Inviting all to seek and bide.

The Workshop of Possibilities

In corners bright with gleaming light,
Ideas bloom, take flight and height.
Crafting dreams with steady hands,
A space where hope and vision stands.

With chisels, tools, and brushes near,
We carve the thoughts we hold most dear.
Each whisper turns to tangible form,
In this warm space where thoughts transform.

Creating worlds from bits and ties,
Where laughter swells and courage flies.
An endless forge of future's spark,
Illuminating paths from dark.

So gather round, let visions reign,
In unity, we'll break the chain.
The workshop calls, its doors are wide,
Step in, embrace the journey's ride.

Mosaic of Whispers and Wills

In colors soft, the stories weave,
A tapestry of dreams we believe.
Each whisper held, a thread so fine,
In every heart, a secret line.

We gather pieces, bold and bright,
Create a vision, pure delight.
With every voice that joins the song,
A mosaic forms, where we belong.

In gentle hues and shades of night,
The will to soar, to claim our light.
Together we will chart the way,
With every breath, a new display.

So let us blend, unite our hearts,
In this grand work, each play our parts.
A canvas rich with life's embrace,
We dance within our shared space.

Celestial Arches of the Mind

Beneath the stars, thoughts intertwine,
Creating arcs where dreams align.
Each sparkle holds a tale untold,
In cosmic realms, our minds behold.

We wander through the starlit skies,
Exploring depths where wisdom lies.
With bouncing light and guiding beams,
We sketch our hopes, we chase our dreams.

The universe reflects our quest,
With every thought, we seek the best.
In celestial heights, our spirits soar,
Unlocking doors to evermore.

So sail the vast, on winds of grace,
In this expanse, we find our place.
The arches stretch, inviting all,
To join the dance, to heed the call.

The Canvas of Dreams

A surface blank, awaiting strokes,
With colors bright, where spirit pokes.
Each vision strikes, a vibrant seed,
In this vast space where heart can lead.

Painted whispers drift on air,
In every hue, a silent prayer.
We blend our souls, the brush in hand,
Creating realms, both wild and grand.

The canvas holds our laughter, tears,
Each layer crafted through our years.
With every stroke, a memory stays,
A portrait formed in myriad ways.

So let us dream, let colors fly,
Together crafted, reaching high.
In this shared space, we are extreme,
A vibrant life, the canvas of dreams.

Bridges Between Realms

Between two worlds, a bridge does gleam,
Connecting dreams that weave their seam.
Whispers of stars, in silence call,
Echoing paths where shadows fall.

Bridges unseen, yet always near,
Carrying hopes, dispelling fear.
Winds of change, they gently sway,
Guiding hearts on their way.

With every step, a tale unfolds,
Of daring deeds and courage bold.
Underneath, the waters flow,
Tales of old and new in tow.

Cross the bridge, let spirits soar,
To realms unknown, forevermore.
A journey starts, with every breath,
In the embrace of life and death.

A Chorus of Invention

In the heart of night, ideas bloom,
Echoing softly, dispelling gloom.
A chorus ring, of voices bright,
   Crafting wonders in the light.

Shapes and forms from dreams arise,
A dance of thought beneath the skies.
Inventive hands and minds so free,
   Together shaping what will be.

The thrill of spark, the clash of steel,
Each creation is a wondrous wheel.
As melodies weave their joyous thread,
   From boundless visions, all are fed.

With courage fierce, we take the stage,
   Living stories, turning the page.
In this vibrant, restless flight,
   Our chorus sings into the night.

The Lighting of Imaginative Fires

Embers flicker in the quiet dark,
A spark awakens, igniting the heart.
From ashes rise, ideas aflame,
Each thought a player in this game.

Gather around, let stories unfold,
Imaginations rich, and bold.
In the heat of night, our minds ignite,
Shedding shadows, embracing light.

The glow of dreams, so vivid, clear,
Warmth of passion, drawing near.
Through the darkness, visions inspire,
With every breath, we breathe this fire.

As flames dance bright, ideas fly,
Painting words across the sky.
In this moment, we are alive,
Together, we dream, together, we thrive.

Veils of Envisioned Realities

In veils of mist, we wander free,
Exploring realms of what could be.
Glimpses of truth, veiled in disguise,
Secrets lurking in endless skies.

Each layer whispers of a new dawn,
A tapestry woven, drawn upon.
Curiosity leads, as we trace,
Paths entwined through time and space.

With each breath, a vision shared,
Brushing against the dreams we've dared.
Veils of enchantment softly part,
Revealing the wonders within the heart.

Embrace the magic, let it unfold,
In possibilities, we are bold.
Reality bends, and we may find,
The veils of dream intertwine with mind.

Milton Keynes UK
Ingram Content Group UK Ltd.
UKHW020703191024
449793UK00005B/36

9 789916 880500